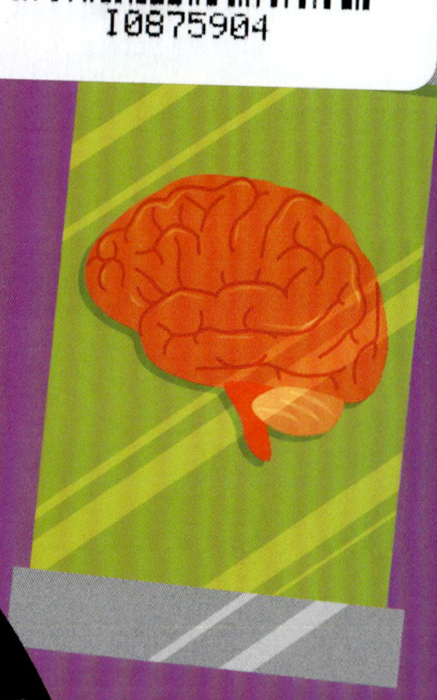

SUPER SMART THINKING

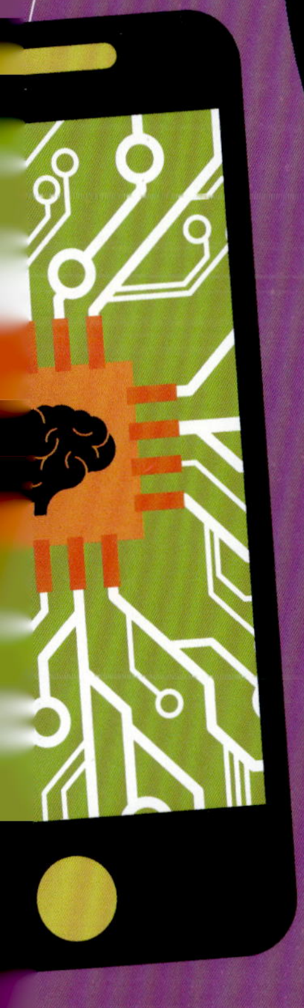

PHILOSOPHY MADE EASY

Written by
Gerald Jones and
Anja Steinbauer

Enslow PUBLISHING

Published in 2027 by Enslow Publishing, LLC
2544 Clinton Street
Buffalo, NY 14224

First published in Great Britain in 2021 by Wayland

Editor: John Hort
Design and illustration: Collaborate Ltd

Printed in China

CPSIA compliance information: Batch #QS27ENS: For further information contact Enslow Publishing LLC, New York, New York at 1-800-398-2504.

Cataloging-in-Publication Data

Names: Jones, Gerald. | Steinbauer, Anja.
Title: Philosophy made easy / by Gerald Jones and Anja Steinbauer.
Description: Buffalo, NY : Enslow Publishing, 2027. | Series: Super smart thinking | Includes glossary and index.
Identifiers: ISBN 9781978549173 (pbk.) | ISBN 9781978549180 (library bound) | ISBN 9781978549197 (ebook)
Subjects: LCSH: Philosophy--Juvenile literature.
Classification: LCC BD31.J66 2027 | DDC 100--dc23

CONTENTS

WHAT IS PHILOSOPHY?

Philosophy is the study of everything we know. The word philosophy means "love" (*philo*) of "wisdom" (*sophia*) in Greek.

Anyone can be a philosopher. You can start philosophizing right now.

ALL YOU NEED ARE THESE THREE THINGS

WONDER

Ancient Greek philosopher Plato (427–347 BCE) said that all philosophy begins with "wonder." This means philosophers are **curious** about the world. They don't simply accept things for what they are, but always ask "why."

REALLY GOOD THINKING

Philosophers are committed to thinking well. They do their best to back up their ideas with good reasons and avoid mistakes.

CONVERSATION

The best way to test your ideas is to discuss them with others. Good philosophical conversations can turn out to be heated discussions but, as Plato reminds us, they have to be carried out with lots of "good will." In other words, a good philosophical **dialogue** is not a competition to "win" the argument, but is about discovering the truth together.

PLATO SHOWED ALL THIS IN HIS ALLEGORY OF THE CAVE

Imagine a group of people living deep down in a cave. They only see shadows on the wall. It is like spending your whole life watching TV. The cave dwellers believe that the shadows are all there is in the world.

One person begins to wonder if this is true. This person is a philosopher – she begins to question what is real and what is not.

As she makes her way up out of the cave, she realises the shadows are just images caused by objects in front of a fire behind the cave dwellers.

Finally, she discovers that there is a whole world outside the cave, with sunlight and real objects. She finds that there is so much to learn.

Thinking about her friends down in the cave, she wants to share her discovery with them. However, they don't believe her and tell her to leave them alone.

As you can see, being a philosopher can be hard, and being a really good philosopher is even harder than it looks. This book is about really good philosophy. Enjoy!

THE BEGINNINGS OF PHILOSOPHY: SOCRATES

Philosophers, like younger brothers or sisters, are always asking questions, particularly "**why**?" and "**what**?". And, just like younger brothers or sisters, this can be a bit annoying. One philosopher called Socrates (ca.470–399 BCE) thought that being irritating was part of his job. He called himself a "gadfly," buzzing around people and stinging them with his questions in order to find out the truth.

Socrates lived over 2,000 years ago in ancient Greece. He was known for being wise. In fact, he was called the "wisest man in the world". But Socrates disagreed with this. He knew he was not a clever politician, or brilliant at business, or skilled in any craft. Socrates believed that he didn't know very much at all – that's why he kept asking questions. And so, he said "if I am wise, it is because I realise that I know nothing."

Socrates asked important philosophical questions that we are still asking today. These are some of the questions we will look at in this book.

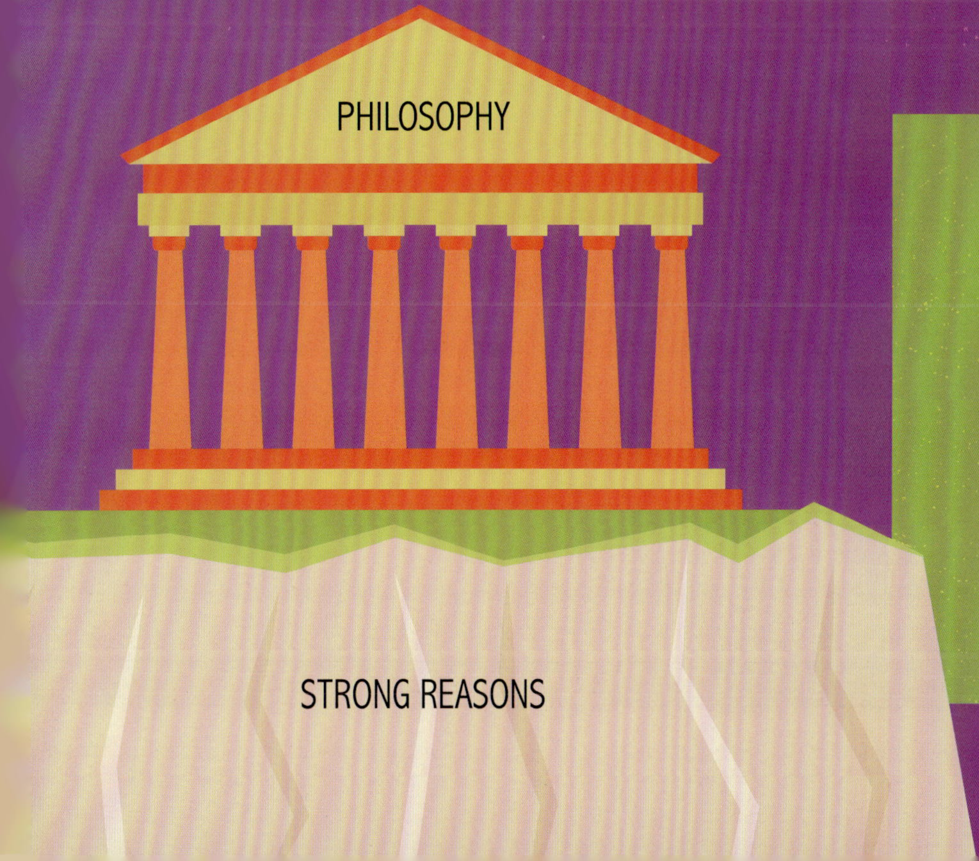

Socrates argued with other people about these questions. He listened carefully to what they said. And he wanted to find the best answers. In philosophy, the best answers are the ones with the strongest **reasons**. So, philosophy is not based on who is the loudest, or who has the most money, or who is the biggest. In philosophy, reason is strength.

THE TOOLS OF PHILOSOPHY: IDEAS AND ARGUMENTS

Philosophers, like scientists, want to understand the world. And they want to find the truth. But philosophers don't have laboratories for doing experiments. They don't have tools like telescopes or microscopes to help them find the answers. The laboratories that philosophers have are in their minds – we call these thought experiments. The tools that philosophers use are words, ideas, and arguments.

One common thought experiment asks this question: How do we know we are not just a brain floating in a tank?

BUILDING AN ARGUMENT

An argument in philosophy is like constructing a building. At the top of the building is an idea or an answer to a question. You are trying to help people get to the top of that building. You want them to believe in your idea, so you give reasons that support your idea.

ARGUMENTS FOR ALIENS

For example, Anja might believe that aliens exist. She gives different reasons for this:

1 Anja has seen some films that have aliens in them (very friendly ones).

2 Anja's best friend said that her cousin's dad flies airplanes, and once he saw an alien spacecraft.

3 Anja has read that there are millions of planets in the universe. She thinks that it is very unlikely that Earth is the only planet with life on it. So she thinks there are probably other planets with life on them.

Some reasons are better than others. For example, films are often just stories, so we shouldn't believe in everything we see in a film. And do you believe everything your best friend tells you? However, the third reason seems more sensible, and is more likely to get people to the top of the building.

THIS PART OF PHILOSOPHY IS CALLED LOGIC OR CRITICAL THINKING.

BELIEVING AND KNOWING

All day long your mind is full of sights, sounds, thoughts, feelings, and **desires**. And it is full of **beliefs**. These are the ideas you have about the world.

Your mind is a very busy place. You hear an ice cream van and you hope it has raspberry ice cream, then you rush toward it, wanting the ice cream.

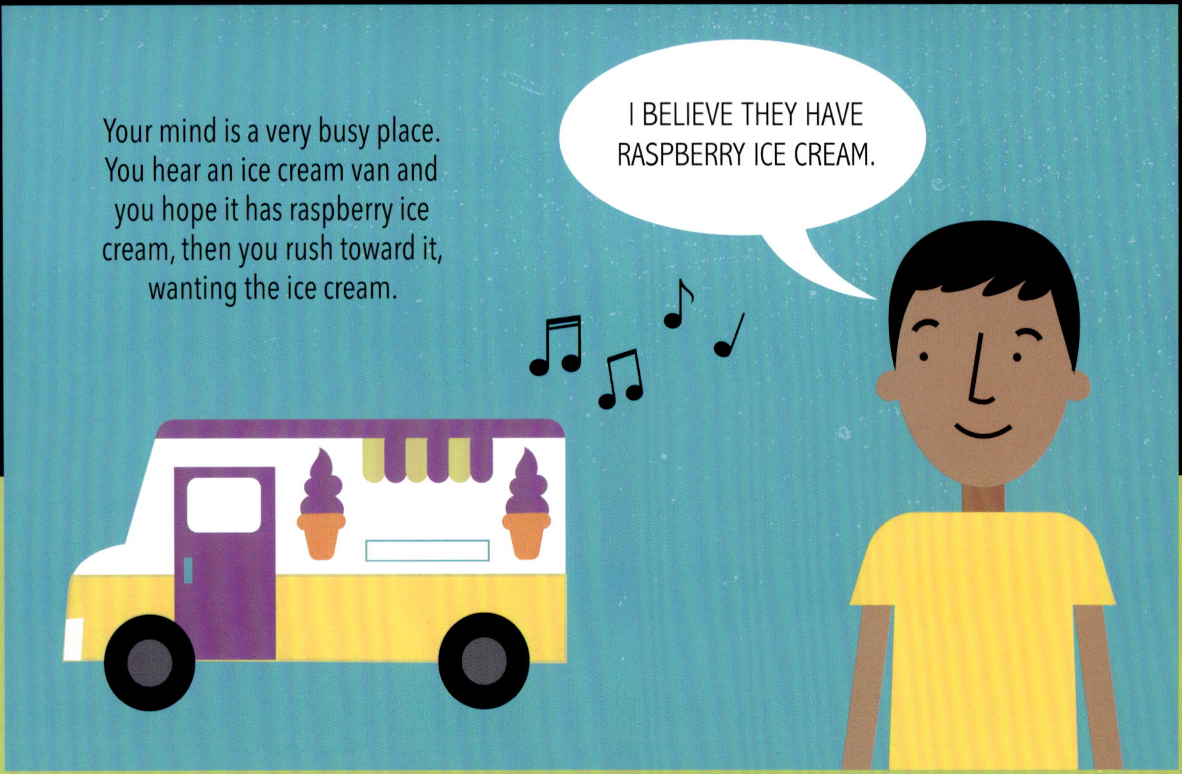

BELIEFS

Philosophers are very interested in beliefs. They could be very important or very boring. You might believe that aliens exist. Or you might believe that you are holding a book right now. Or you might believe that this is the 21st century. Or you might believe that there are millions of stars in the universe.

A belief is an idea you have about what is true. And a belief is also something that makes you move and take action. For example, you have reason to believe that the van has raspberry ice cream (you had one yesterday and the day before!), but they might have run out, so you walk to the van. And, phew, there is raspberry ice cream!

Five minutes ago, you could say only, "I believe they have raspberry ice cream." But now you can shout out, "I KNOW they have raspberry ice cream!" You have seen it with your own eyes. Philosophers have been interested in knowledge since the time of Socrates. Philosophers often say a belief that is true, and based on reasons, is called knowledge.

Philosophers want to look closely at what we believe and what we know. They investigate to see whether our beliefs are true. And they want to see whether our beliefs are based on good reasons.

THIS PART OF PHILOSOPHY IS CALLED EPISTEMOLOGY.

DOUBT AND THE FOUNDATIONS OF KNOWLEDGE

How can we know if our beliefs are true? Imagine you have a large barrel of apples. You are worried that some of the apples might be rotten. So you tip them all out onto a table and check them one by one. A philosopher called René Descartes (1596–1650) thought he should do the same thing with his beliefs. He thought the best way to check his beliefs was by doubting them. In other words, he was asking himself, "Could this belief be wrong?"

I THINK THEREFORE I AM

Descartes found that he could doubt nearly all of his beliefs. But there was one thing he couldn't doubt! He couldn't doubt that he, Descartes, existed. Because whenever he tried to doubt he existed, he realised that he, Descartes, was the person doing the doubting. So he famously said, "Whenever I think or doubt, then I know I must exist." Or, in a shorter sentence, "I think therefore I am." Descartes thought he had finally found a firm foundation for his knowledge. However, beyond this, knowledge becomes more difficult to define.

WHERE DOES KNOWLEDGE COME FROM?

Some philosophers think that knowledge must come from experience. When you were born you didn't know anything. You hadn't yet had any experiences. A baby's mind is like a blank piece of paper, waiting to be written on. As you get older you experience more of the world through looking and hearing and touching what is around you. And so perhaps knowledge comes only from our senses.

2 + 2 = 4 ✓

1. SOCRATES IS A MAN
2. ALL MEN ARE MORTAL
3. SOCRATES IS MORTAL ✓

Other philosophers disagree. They think our senses can be wrong – there are many examples of people being mistaken about what they see or hear. They argue that genuine knowledge must come from the mind (for example, the truths of math and **logic**). It is not possible to doubt that 2+2 = 4. We can know this is true without using our senses.

THIS DEBATE IS BETWEEN EMPIRICISTS AND RATIONALISTS; EMPIRICISTS BELIEVE KNOWLEDGE IS BASED ON EXPERIENCE GAINED FROM THE SENSES, WHEREAS RATIONALISTS BELIEVE KNOWLEDGE COMES FROM REASON.

EXISTENCE AND REALITY

Some of the questions that philosophers ask seem small. Questions like: How do we know that van has raspberry ice cream? But often philosophical questions are huge. They are about life, the universe, and everything: is there a god? How free are we? Is there life after death? Who am I? Perhaps you have wondered about a question like this.

These questions are about the world. But they are not questions that scientists can answer. They go beyond experience and beyond **physics**. Philosophers want to understand and describe the real world beyond our senses.

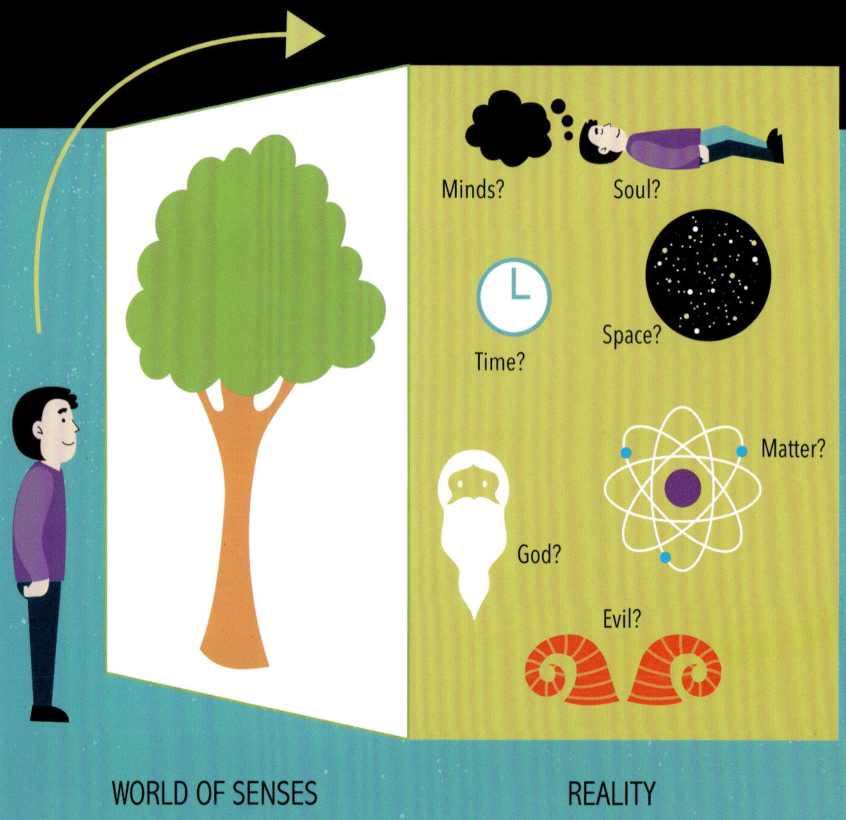

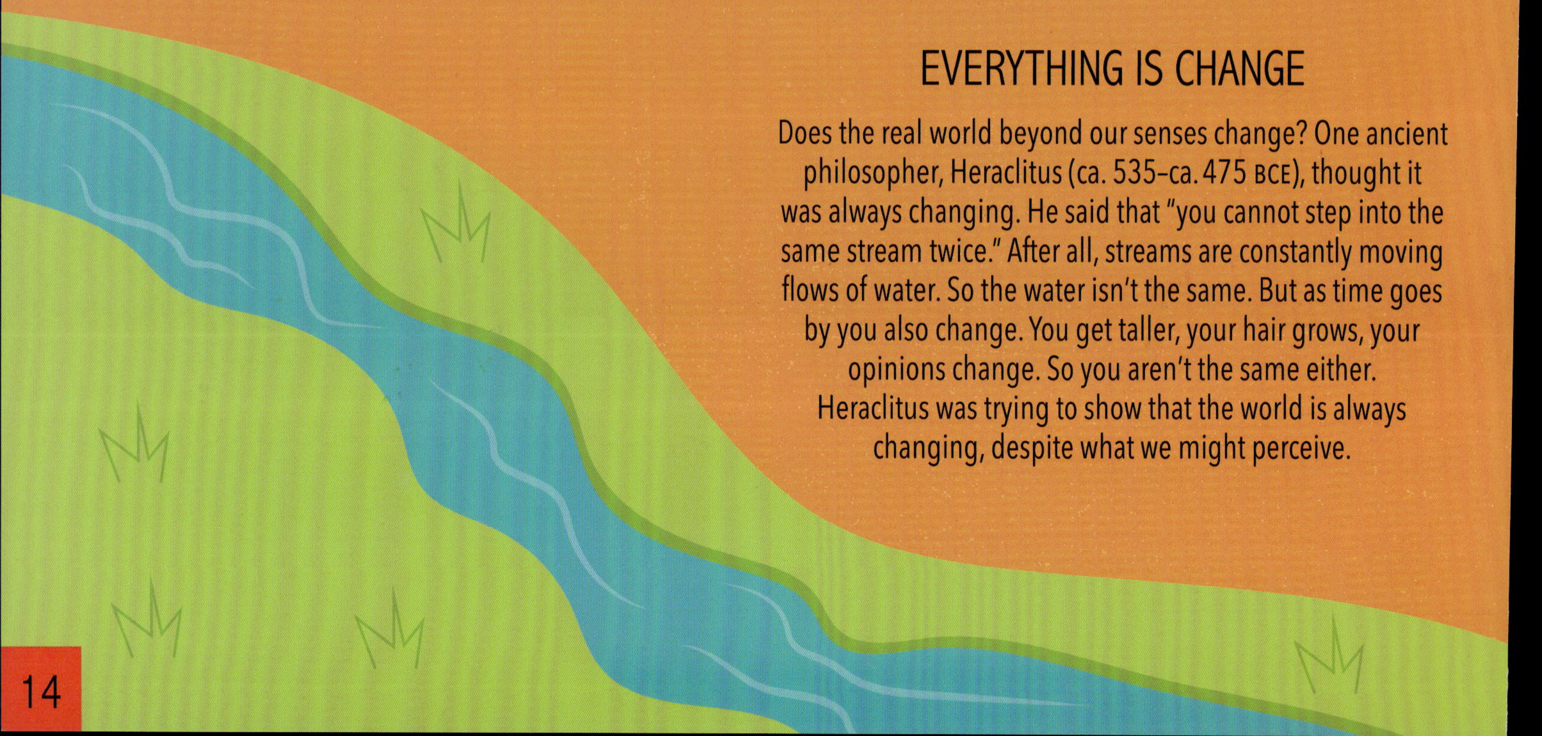

EVERYTHING IS CHANGE

Does the real world beyond our senses change? One ancient philosopher, Heraclitus (ca. 535–ca. 475 BCE), thought it was always changing. He said that "you cannot step into the same stream twice." After all, streams are constantly moving flows of water. So the water isn't the same. But as time goes by you also change. You get taller, your hair grows, your opinions change. So you aren't the same either. Heraclitus was trying to show that the world is always changing, despite what we might perceive.

CHANGE AS AN ILLUSION

Another ancient philosopher, Zeno (ca. 495–ca. 430 BCE), thought that change was impossible. We see change around us, but this is an illusion of our sense. The real world (beyond our senses) actually stays the same.

SOME PHILOSOPHERS TALK ABOUT THE VEIL OF PERCEPTION, THE IDEA THAT EVERYTHING OUR SENSES DETECT IS A VEIL THAT HIDES THE REAL WORLD.

Zeno gave a thought experiment to show this. Imagine an athlete chasing a tortoise. The tortoise starts moving. The athlete runs forward and closes the gap by a half. The tortoise moves forward. The athlete runs and closes the gap by another half (a quarter of the original distance). The tortoise moves forward. The athlete closes the gap by another half (1/8 of the original distance). And so on. Every time the athlete moves forward, the tortoise always moves forward. This argument suggests that the athlete would never reach the tortoise. We see movement, but for Zeno this is an illusion.

THIS PART OF PHILOSOPHY, WHICH DEALS WITH ABSTRACT CONCEPTS, IS CALLED METAPHYSICS.

DOES GOD EXIST?

One day you may be lucky enough to really see the stars at night – away from the streetlights of our towns and roads. The sight is dizzying. Thousands of stars fill the sky, with millions beyond, and they inspire wonder. Why are we here? What created all of this? What is our purpose? These are questions humans have always asked. And for many people the existence of God provides an answer.

WHAT IS GOD?

It is helpful to understand what people mean by "God." A god (or the singular God) is a being who exists outside the universe. God is usually thought of as all-powerful and all-knowing, a being who can do anything and who knows everything. And God is often thought of as the all-loving creator of everything.

How do people know that God exists? Many people say they experience God in their lives as a calming presence or as a guide. Some people even say they have seen or heard God. There are arguments for and against God's existence.

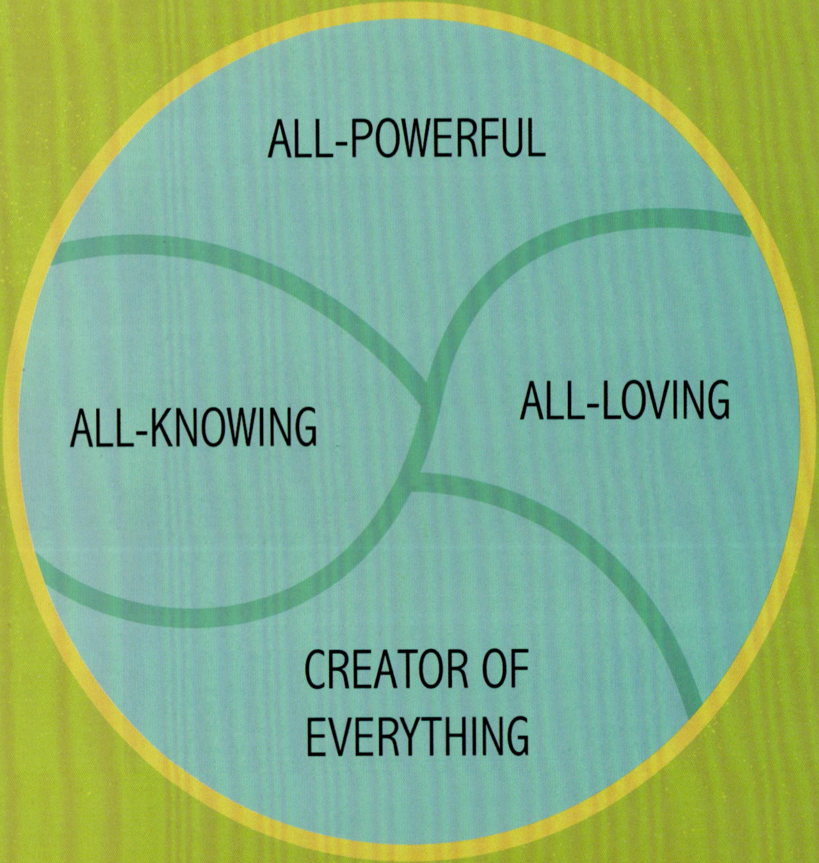

THE TELEOLOGICAL ARGUMENT

One argument for the existence of God is called "the design argument," sometimes known as "the teleological argument." It suggests that when we look very closely at the world, it all seems to fit together perfectly, a bit like a machine. For example, the way an animal's eye works is extremely complicated. It also looks as if the world has physical laws and is full of order. Only a powerful designer, like a god, could have a created a world like this.

However, the teleological argument has its critics. Scientific theories, such as evolution by natural selection, can explain the existence of animal eyes, and biology can even show the world is not perfect – some animals are born blind, for instance. The universe can also be seen as a chaotic place; just because there are physical laws dictating it does not mean it has been designed.

THE COSMOLOGICAL ARGUMENT

Some people believe that the fact that the universe exists is proof that God exists. The universe cannot have appeared from nothing. So something, such as God, must have triggered the universe into motion. This is known as "the cosmological argument."

However, some people argue that the cosmological argument only defers the problem – if God existed before the universe, who created God? Or is it possible that God doesn't "exist" in a way we understand, and didn't need to be created?

THE PROBLEM OF EVIL

An argument against a god is called "the problem of evil." There is so much pain and suffering in the world. Animals die in forest fires. Humans kill each other. We suffer from diseases. So, some philosophers say this is evidence that there is no God or that God is not all-powerful, or is not all-knowing, or is not loving.

However, some religious philosophers argue that evil is not the fault of God, but the price of God giving people free will. If we are free to think, act, and move around as much as we like, God cannot be held responsible for our actions and consequences. Instead, it is we who are responsible for our own actions, both good and bad.

THIS PART OF PHILOSOPHY IS CALLED THE PHILOSOPHY OF RELIGION.

MIND AND IDENTITY: WHO ARE YOU?

French philosopher René Descartes said: "I think therefore I am" (see page 12). So, in some sense, who I am has to do with the fact that I think.

However, our ways of thinking can change. You don't think the same way you used to when you were a toddler. You don't have the same interests, likes, and dislikes. Our minds have changed. What does it mean to still be you from day to day? Philosophers call this the problem of identity.

As we get older our thoughts and bodies change.

As you can see, the question of identity is connected to the problem of change. Wearing different clothes, getting a haircut, or learning to play the piano are changes, but it seems they don't change you enough to change who you are.

HOW MUCH CHANGE CAN YOU SURVIVE AND STILL BE THE SAME PERSON?

Ancient Greek philosophers discussed this problem using a thought experiment: The Ship of Theseus.

After many adventurous voyages, the ship of the great Greek hero Theseus is in a bad state of disrepair. Many parts of it need to be replaced. As time goes on, all the parts get replaced. Is this still the same ship?

What if a clever shipbuilder uses the discarded planks from Theseus's old ship to build a new ship? Which is then the ship of Theseus?

HOW FREE ARE WE?

What is freedom? Is it the opposite to being a prisoner?
Or the ability to do whatever you like?

Many philosophers think freedom is connected with making choices.

Life is full of choices, and often it seems obvious to us that we can freely choose whatever we like. For example, you can choose if you are going to have strawberry or a chocolate ice cream on a hot day, as long as both are available and you can pay for them.

There are some choices that you cannot make, such as choosing to lift off from your chair and fly around the room. This is because gravity and the fact that humans are not physically equipped to fly make this adventure impossible. There are other factors that limit what we can choose, such as time, money, the law, and our parents or teachers.

SO, AS HUMANS, WE ARE NOT ABSOLUTELY FREE TO MAKE ALL THE CHOICES WE MIGHT LIKE TO MAKE.

However, you might say, we can still choose ice creams, books, hobbies, careers, friends, clothes, and many other things, large and small.

Some philosophers argue that we may not be as free as it seems to us. They say that we are part of nature. What happens in nature is determined by the laws of nature and can be predicted before it happens. So, this must be true of us too. This idea is called determinism.

For example, think of an uncaged bird. The bird can fly wherever it likes, it can eat, sleep, or sing whenever it chooses. Surely, it is therefore free? However, the bird will act on instinct, eat, and sleep when necessary, not when it chooses.

When we choose what to eat, how to dress, or what to do, we may have as little freedom as the bird. Our upbringing, personality, and nature might decide for us.

There are plenty of philosophers who believe that the truth lies somewhere in the middle, that we are neither fully free, nor totally determined. Other philosophers think that we might be free and determined at the same time.

LIVING TOGETHER: WHAT IS POLITICS?

Politics is about living together in a community. There are many issues that need to be settled before this can work well. You probably know this from your family life. You might have particular responsibilities, such as cleaning your room; rights, such as using a tablet; and particular freedoms, such as choosing how to spend your free time. Other members of your family might have different responsibilities, rights, and freedoms. Making all this work is not always easy.

The great Greek philosopher Aristotle (384–322 BCE) believed that humans want to live together, and are naturally well equipped to settle all the issues that we need to settle in order to do so. In fact, true happiness can only be found in our common lives.

The German philosopher Arthur Schopenhauer (1788–1860 CE) thought that humans need to live together but they are not altogether happy doing so. Schopenhauer told the story of the porcupines to show what he means.

On a cold day, a number of porcupines huddle together for warmth. However, soon they have to disperse again because they start pricking each other with their quills. But then the cold drives them back together. In this way, they keep coming together and dispersing, again and again. Humans, Schopenhauer thought, are just like that. We need each other and our lives are safer and better in a community. But when we get too close to each other we start arguing and getting on each other's nerves, so we keep our distance again, before we need each other and come back together.

WHO IS RIGHT?

Aristotle, who thinks the company of others makes us happy and makes our lives meaningful, or Schopenhauer, who believes that living with others is always difficult or even unpleasant?

MORAL MATTERS: WHAT SHOULD I DO?

Morals are the **principles** we have for what is right and wrong. From early childhood onwards, we are told that we should be good. But what does this actually mean? And why should we be good? Philosophers like Aristotle think that we need to be good people for two reasons:

1. IT MAKES LIVING WITH OTHERS MUCH MORE PLEASANT

2. WE CAN BE HAPPIER WITH OURSELVES

It is raining outside. Isla has brought an umbrella, but Alex has not. Alex tells himself that he could easily "borrow" the umbrella without Isla noticing and return it to her tomorrow. True, Isla would get wet on her way home. But, he thinks, if one of them can stay dry, it might as well be him. Is it wrong for Alex to take Isla's umbrella? Why?

WHY SHOULD WE BE GOOD?

German philosopher Immanuel Kant (1724–1804) said that when we think about what we should do, we should imagine what it would be like if everybody acted in this way. It may seem like a good idea to Alex to take the umbrella. But if we think about what it would be like if everybody took whatever they liked whenever they liked, even if they returned it, we can see that it would turn out to be a world where you can never really trust anyone. Everyone could just do what was good for them.

Maybe, given a chance, we would all act selfishly all the time.

HERE IS A STORY THAT EXPLAINS THIS:

In one of Plato's books, the philosopher Glaucon tells us the story of the ring of Gyges.

Gyges was a shepherd. One day he finds a mysterious ring. He discovers that the ring has the power to turn him invisible. Gyges was not a particularly bad person to start with, but eventually he uses the ring to commit a number of crimes until he becomes king.

Glaucon believes that if you had two such rings and you gave one to a good person and one to a bad person, both would end up doing bad things. Such power is just too hard to resist.

Glaucon says we are good people only because we know that if we do bad things we might get caught. Is that true? What would you do if you had the magic ring?

THIS PART OF PHILOSOPHY IS CALLED ETHICS.

ART AND BEAUTY

When you see a rose, you might comment, "The rose is red." This is a matter of knowledge and judgment.

But something very different happens when we say, "The rose is beautiful."

What is that difference? Is saying that the rose is beautiful just as obvious as saying that it is red? Some people would say that while we can all agree that it is red, we may disagree about it being beautiful.

Philosophers wonder what makes us say that something is beautiful. There are two possibilities:

1

Perhaps beauty is in the object itself; perhaps it is to do with having really good proportions, colors, or harmonies. This means that when we disagree about something being beautiful, one of us is right and the other person is wrong.

2

On the other hand, maybe we disagree about what is beautiful because things aren't actually beautiful or ugly. We just see them as such. It depends on what we happen to like. So when you say, "This music is beautiful," you're not actually saying anything other than "I like this music."

THE POWER OF ART

Plato was worried about art and beauty. He thought that it could change the way we feel about things, and because it could change the way we feel, it could change the way we act. For example, if you play soft, sad violin music to someone who is meant to fight in a boxing match, it might make them cry, and they won't want to go out and fight. Sometimes, this can be used for a good purpose, such as when pictures of cute animals make people more concerned about animal welfare. Plato was worried, however, that we could be manipulated by art and beauty, and he thought this was wrong, even if it was for a good cause.

Aristotle disagreed with Plato – he thought that art and beauty were important in our lives. The feelings they inspire make us more human and help us learn about ourselves.

Some philosophers believe that art and beauty can make us happier and better. What do you think? What would life be like without music, fashion, or beauty?

THE BRANCH OF PHILOSOPHY WHERE WE THINK ABOUT ART AND BEAUTY IS CALLED AESTHETICS.

THE FUTURE OF PHILOSOPHY

Philosophy can and should be about anything that matters to us. We use it to tell good arguments from bad ones and to come to well-grounded conclusions.

Therefore, philosophy is very useful to help us think about the problems of our time.

For example, we need to think more about the nature of **AI**. Philosophers wonder whether computers can think. Can we perhaps even say that the human mind is like a computer? How can we program self-driving cars to make the right decisions in case of a possible accident? Can robots be good companions for people who are lonely and vulnerable?

Here is another example: A major problem of our time is climate change. Philosophy has much to say about this issue. Philosophers discuss questions such as "Whose responsibility is it to reduce the greenhouse effect?" or "To what degree do we have to change our lives to fight climate change?"

We need to come up with better and better answers.

HERE IS AN EXAMPLE:

We share a world in which we must decide who gets what, and who can or must do what. Philosophers think of these questions as concerning **justice**. Philosopher John Rawls (1921–2002) explains that "justice" is the same as "fairness." This is very helpful but still doesn't tell us enough about what is fair in any given situation.

It is a hot day. Oscar, Phoebe, and Sharel decide to make fresh lemonade. Sharel buys the lemons, and Oscar mixes all the ingredients. Phoebe doesn't really help, but says that she is particularly thirsty. How should the lemonade be split up between them? Perhaps Phoebe should not get anything because she didn't help? Or should Sharel and Oscar get more because they put money and work into the process? On the other hand, does Phoebe have a right to a bigger glass because she is so thirsty? Maybe they should all get an equal amount?

What is fair? Also, who should decide? Do all three of them need to agree? Should Sharel decide because these are his lemons? Should they call someone else, maybe a parent, to make the decision for them?

All of these questions are ones that communities must answer. Here it is not about lemonade, but about money, opportunities, and power, but also punishments.

Who deserves what? Who has a right to expect help or privileges, such as education? Are all members of a society equal?

AS YOU CAN SEE, THERE IS PLENTY OF WORK TO DO FOR THE PHILOSOPHERS OF THE FUTURE, PHILOSOPHERS LIKE YOU!

GLOSSARY

Abstract
Something that is based on thoughts and ideas rather than things that exist or are definite

AI
Stands for artificial intelligence, computers programmed to perform tasks in a way that mimics human thought

Allegory
A story that has a meaning within it; it can be to explain an idea or lesson

Belief
Something that you accept as true, sometimes without proof or certainty that it is

Cosmological
Relating to the origins and development of the universe

Critical thinking
Using facts and evidence to reach a conclusion

Curious
Eager to know more about something

Desire
A strong feeling of want

Dialogue
Discussion between two or more parties

Doubt
A feeling of uncertainty about something

Epistemology
The theory or study of knowledge

Harmonies
When different elements work well together, rather than clashing

Justice
Being fair, or treated in a reasonable way

Logic
Thinking based on reasons and facts

Morals
A standard of behavior based on (principles of) right or wrong

Perception
What we are able to see or hear, or are aware of through our senses

Physics
The science of the physical world, particularly energy and matter

Principles
Rules or beliefs that help you decide how to behave

Reality
Things that actually exist

Reason
An explanation for an action or event

Teleological
Understanding things by their purpose rather than their origins

FURTHER INFORMATION

BOOKS

Sophie's World by Jostein Gaarder (Orion Children's Books, 1991)

What is Politics? Why Should we Care? And Other Big Questions by Michael Rosen and Annemarie Young (Wayland, 2019)

What is Right and Wrong? Who Decides? Where Do Values Come From? And Other Big Questions by Michael Rosen and Annemarie Young (Wayland, 2018)

WEBSITES

kids.britannica.com/kids/article/philosophy/399564
This website has lots of information on philosophy and related topics.

www.philosophy-foundation.org/resources-for-children
The website for the Philosophy Foundation includes resources for children.

INDEX